Your skin, your eyes, your beautiful hair,

And though you are beautiful beyond measure,

keep in mind that your brain is your greatest treasure.

Black Girls grow up into strong Black Women

Sojourner, Coretta, Harriet, and Gwen...

our presence is visible now because of who they were then.

Rosa, Michelle, Eartha, Serena, too.

Black Girls, let these powerful women inspire you.

Stand up, take your place, raise your hand, and claim your crowns

Only you define you and the story you have to tell.

They may say to you, "No," but keep your spirit pointed at, "Yes."

Look in the mirror and say,
"I love you, each and every part."

www.ingramcontent.com/pod-product-compliance
Lightning Source LLC
Chambersburg PA
CBHW060306010526
44108CB00041B/2585